Christmas Maths
for ages 9–11

Andrew Brodie ✓

Content of the worksheets

The first section of the book (Worksheets 1–22) contains activities that are targeted towards Year 5, while the later pages (Worksheets 23–44) are targeted towards Year 6. However, you may decide to use any of the sheets with your own class, regardless of which year groups you have. The aim should be for pupils to be engaged in enjoyable activities that provide practice of mathematical skills and knowledge.

Year 5

Worksheet		Objective
1	Double the presents!	Mental calculations using known number facts; use doubling and halving.
2	Doubling tree	Mental calculations using known number facts; use doubling and halving.
3	Christmas lights	Mental calculations using known number facts; use doubling and halving; know by heart all multiplication facts up to 10 X 10.
4	Christmas code	Learn the doubles of all whole numbers up to 100
5	Santa's stock check (1)	Place value; ordering and rounding; use the vocabulary of comparing and ordering numbers including symbols such as < and >.
6	Santa's stock check (2)	Place value; ordering and rounding; use the vocabulary of comparing and ordering numbers including symbols such as < and >.
7	Santa's stock check (3)	Place value; ordering and rounding; subtraction.
8	Christmas puzzle (1)	Understand number facts and place value for mental addition and subtraction
9	Christmas puzzle (2)	Understand number facts and place value for mental addition and subtraction
10	Taking measurements (1)	Measure the perimeter and area of simple shapes
11	Taking measurements (2)	Measure the perimeter and area of simple shapes
12	Christmas coordinates	Read and plot coordinates in the first quadrant
13	A cold, cold Christmas (1)	Recognise and use negative numbers in the context of temperature; use vocabulary related to time.
14	A cold, cold Christmas (2)	Recognise and use negative numbers in the context of temperature; use vocabulary related to time.
15	Christmas multiples	Properties of number sequences
16	Christmas Town	Properties of number sequences
17	Match the presents	Change an improper fraction to a mixed number
18	Feeding the reindeer	Recognise when two simple fractions are equivalent
19	Cooking the turkey (1)	Solve simple problems involving ratio
20	Cooking the turkey (2)	Solve simple problems involving ratio
21	Counting the days (1)	Understand time on calendars; spell days of the week.
22	Counting the days (2)	Understand time on calendars; spell days of the week.

Year 6

Worksheet		Objective
23	Christmas visitors (1)	Solve problems involving money and measures
24	Christmas visitors (2)	Solve problems involving money and measures
25	Christmas visitors (3)	Solve problems involving money and measures
26	Christmas visitors (4)	Solve problems involving money and measures
27	Christmas visitors (5)	Solve problems involving money and measures
28	Santa's workshop (1)	Begin to find the mean of a set of data
29	Santa's workshop (2)	Begin to find the mean of a set of data
30	Oh Christmas tree!	Find differences by counting up; use informal pencil and paper methods to record additions and subtractions.
31	Complete the puzzle (1)	Understand percentage as the number of parts per hundred and find simple percentages of numbers
32	Complete the puzzle (2)	Understand percentage as the number of parts per hundred and find simple percentages of numbers
33	The twelve days of Christmas (1)	'Using and applying' mathematical skills; properties of numbers and number sequences; calculation strategies, both mental and written; solve problems.
34	The twelve days of Christmas (2)	'Using and applying' mathematical skills; properties of numbers and number sequences; calculation strategies, both mental and written; solve problems.
35	The twelve days of Christmas (3)	'Using and applying' mathematical skills; properties of numbers and number sequences; calculation strategies, both mental and written; solve problems.
36	Treats for Santa (1)	Use, read and write standard metric measures; solve problems including 'real life' money or measures.
37	Treats for Santa (2)	Use, read and write standard metric measures; solve problems including 'real life' money or measures.
38	Treats for Santa (3)	Use, read and write standard metric measures; solve problems including 'real life' money or measures.
39	Chocolate decorations	Multiply whole numbers by 10, 100; use multiplication to solve word problems involving money.
40	Christmas stars	Recognise number sequences and patterns.
41	The 25th of December	Solve mathematical problems; recognise and explain patterns and relationships.
42	2007 Calendar	Read the time from calendars; use vocabulary related to time; know the number of days in each month.
43	2008 Calendar	Read the time from calendars; use vocabulary related to time; know the number of days in each month.
44	My calendar	Read the time from calendars; use vocabulary related to time; know the number of days in each month.

Andrew Brodie: Christmas Maths 9–11 © A & C Black Publishers Ltd. 2006

Worksheet 1 — Double the presents!

Name:  Date:

Look at this number sequence:

1, 2, 4, 8, 16, 32, 64, 128, 256, 512

Can you see the pattern? Starting at 1, each number that follows is double the number preceding it.

Follow the instructions below to colour the presents on the sleigh.

1. Colour green the number 1 and the nine following doubles.
2. Colour yellow the number 3 and the nine following doubles.
3. Colour orange the number 5 and the nine following doubles.
4. Colour blue all other numbered parcels.
5. Now you can colour the rest of the picture.

Numbers on parcels: 1, 384, 765, 24, 160, 20, 96, 80, 8, 512, 640, 1280, 32, 45, 768, 128, 3, 51, 320, 64, 103, 40, 5, 4, 10, 12, 87, 697, 192, 2, 6, 93, 256, 48, 643, 2560, 461, 45, 907, 16, 1536

Notes for teachers
Objective: Mental calculations using known number facts; using doubling and halving.
Encourage pupils to notice the relationship between the doubles that start on 1 and those that start on 5 (from 10 onwards in the '5' string each number is ten times that of the '1' string). Also help them to see that after the first number in each string there are only even numbers.

Andrew Brodie: Christmas Maths 9–11 © A & C Black Publishers Ltd. 2006

Doubling tree

Name:    Date:

Follow the instructions below to colour the decorations on the tree.

1. Colour red the number 7 and the nine following doubles.
2. Colour yellow the number 9 and the nine following doubles.
3. Colour orange the number 11 and the nine following doubles.
4. Colour blue all other numbered decorations.
5. Now you can colour the tree and the rest of the picture.

Notes for teachers
Objective: Mental calculations using known number facts; using doubling and halving.
If pupils have understood the activity on Worksheet 1, they may choose to colour the 'extra' decorations in blue before finding the appropriate doubles as they will be able to appreciate that all odd numbers apart from the start number should be blue. An extension to this activity would be to give pupils a sheet with a large plain Christmas tree shape and invite them to make a numbered tree with instructions for another pupil to colour. This could, for example, be doubling from a different starting point, colouring based on multiplication tables, etc.

Andrew Brodie: Christmas Maths 9–11 © A & C Black Publishers Ltd. 2006

Christmas lights

Name:  Date:

Look at this number sequence: **968, 484, 242, 121**

Can you see the pattern? Starting at 968, each number that follows is half the number preceding it.

The lights in the sky need to be coloured correctly by following the instructions below.

1. Colour yellow 968 and the following 3 halves.
2. Colour red 288 and the following 5 halves.
3. Colour pink 480 and the following 5 halves.
4. Leave white the remaining lights.
5. Now look at the houses below. Colour the houses with numbers in the 11 times table blue, those in the 9 times table green and those in the 7 times table purple.

Notes for teachers
Objective: Mental calculations using known number facts; using doubling and halving; know by heart all multiplication facts up to 10 X 10.
Encourage pupils to notice that the white lights are also a doubling/halving string. Ask pupils why they think each of the given strings finishes with an odd number – this could lead to exploring the continuation of the halving, including fractions.

Christmas code

Name:  Date:

Double each number in the coded message below to find out which letter it represents. The first word has been done for you.
Notice that each letter has three possible code numbers.

```
A 22, 86, 190        H 34, 104, 170       O 26,  52, 154      V 12, 146, 194
B 38, 184, 200       I 16, 134, 158       P 40,  82, 182      W 44, 108, 186
C 28, 58, 126        J 30,  98, 198       Q 36,  88, 192      X  4,  84, 140
D 70, 142, 188       K  8, 114, 144       R 10,  76, 150      Y 60, 118, 164
E 66, 68, 94         L  2, 100, 180       S 48, 152, 196      Z 14,  80, 174
F 50, 112, 156       M 18,  78, 178       T 46, 102, 168
G 20, 64, 130        N 32, 132, 162       U  6,  24, 160
```

32 13 77 71   72 8 81 65   22 33 16 29 34 98 1 43 76
64 26 154 142   __ __ __ __   __ __ __ __ __ __ __ __ __
G O O D

49 8 16 10 50 47   100 34 90 2 24
__ __ __ __ __ __   __ __ __ __ __
__ __ __ __ __ __   __ __ __ __ __

67 81   23 52 33   100 50 47 11 57   9 8 71 22 79 16 84 34 75
__ __   __ __ __   __ __ __ __ __   __ __ __ __ __ __ __ __ __

Notes for teachers
Objective: Learn the doubles of all whole numbers up to 100
Pupils can use this code to work out the numbers they would need to give to other pupils for more Christmas carol lines. This would give them halving practice to match the doubling they have been doing.

Andrew Brodie: Christmas Maths 9–11 © A & C Black Publishers Ltd. 2006

Worksheet 5: Santa's stock check (1)

Name:  Date:

Santa needs to keep track of roughly how many gifts are available for him to deliver this year.

Look at the stock figures below. Write the name of the correct gift in the table. The first one has been done for you.

 Electronic games 9,650

 Woolly hats 16,249

Art sets 4,924

18,000 <	books	< 20,000
7,600 <	_____	< 7,700
9,990 <	_____	< 10,309
11,295 <	_____	< 12,700
12,300 <	_____	< 14,432
3,999 <	_____	< 4,999
6,000 <	_____	< 7,500
9,649 <	_____	< 9,651
15,000 <	_____	< 17,000

 Books 19,653

 Watches 6,256

 Skates 10,308

 Footballs 12,738

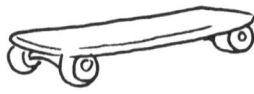 Skateboards 7,627

 Board games 11,498

Notes for teachers
Objective: Place value; ordering and rounding; use the vocabulary of comparing and ordering numbers including symbols such as < and >.
For many pupils the inequality signs are very difficult to use. This task uses them in a context that is both imaginary and realistic and provides an excellent aid to understanding. Those pupils who find the task straightforward could move on quickly to Worksheets 6 and 7. Answers on page 48.

Andrew Brodie: Christmas Maths 9–11 © A & C Black Publishers Ltd. 2006

Santa's stock check (2)

Name: Date:

Check the number of each item. Arrange them in order on the table from the least to the most.

Complete the table by rounding to the nearest ten, the nearest hundred and the nearest thousand. The first one has been done for you.

 Electronic games 9,650    Woolly hats 16,249   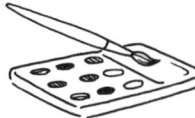 Art sets 4,924

 Books 19,653    Watches 6,256    Skates 10,308

 Footballs 12,738   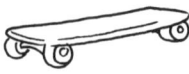 Skateboards 7,627    Board games 11,498

Item	Number	Rounded to nearest 10	Rounded to nearest 100	Rounded to nearest 1000
Art Sets	4,924	4,920	4,900	5,000

Notes for teachers
Objective: Place value; ordering and rounding; use the vocabulary of comparing and ordering numbers including symbols such as < & >.
When rounding to the nearest hundred or the nearest thousand the children may need to be reminded that they are rounding from the number of items not from the previously rounded figure. So, for example there are 11,498 board games which rounds to 11,500 to the nearest ten or hundred but only rounds to 11,000 to the nearest thousand. Answers on page 48.

Santa's stock check (3)

Name:  Date:

This year Santa needs 20,000 of each item. Calculate how many more of each item he will need to make. Show how you worked each of them out.

Board games 11,498 + _____ = 20,000

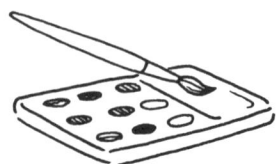 Art sets 4,924+ _____ = 20,000

Books 19,653 + _____ = 20,000

 Electronic games 9,650+ _____ = 20,000

Footballs 12,738 + _____ = 20,000

 Watches 6,256+ _____ = 20,000

Skates 10,308+ _____ = 20,000

 Woolly hats 16,249 + _____ =20,000

Notes for teachers
Objective: Place value; ordering and rounding; subtraction.
The pupils should not use calculators but can use a variety of mental or written methods to solve these subtractions. See page 48 for correct answers. An additional task could be to ask children what type of maths they could set for others to complete from the stock numbers on this sheet.

Christmas puzzle (1)

Name:  Date:

Cut out the square puzzle pieces. Each one has a number on it.

The answer to each of the calculations on Worksheet 9 will show you where to stick the pieces to complete the picture.

Notes for teachers
Objective: Understand number facts and place value for mental addition and subtraction
This page needs to be used in conjunction with Worksheet 9 as it contains the answers to the questions on Worksheet 9.

Andrew Brodie: Christmas Maths 9–11 © A & C Black Publishers Ltd. 2006

Worksheet 9: Christmas puzzle (2)

Name:  Date:

7.7 – 6.6	6.7 – 3.3	10.7 – 8.7	1.6 – 1.5	1.9 + 2.1
6.8 + 3.2	2.7 + 2.3	10.4 – 9.4	3.9 + 3.1	5.5 + 4.1
5.5 + 5.4	6.1 + 3.1	11.4 – 0.7	5.2 + 3.0	10.7 – 6.2
7.3 – 5.2	4.5 + 4.5	1.8 + 2.6	7.2 + 1.3	1.6 + 1.5
8.3 – 2.6	1.9 + 1.9	7.8 + 0.3	10.1 – 5.2	7.2 – 1.3
0.5 + 1.7	4.2 – 1.2	2.2 + 4.4	6.4 – 0.4	6.3 + 2.5
9.5 – 1.5	12.7 – 10.1	9.9 – 6.6	2.6 + 2.6	2.7 + 3.7

Notes for teachers
Objective: Understand number facts and place value for mental addition and subtraction
An extension to this activity could be for pupils to use Christmas pictures (perhaps old Christmas cards) to create their own puzzle pictures for other pupils to complete.

Worksheet 10

Taking measurements (1)

Name: Date:

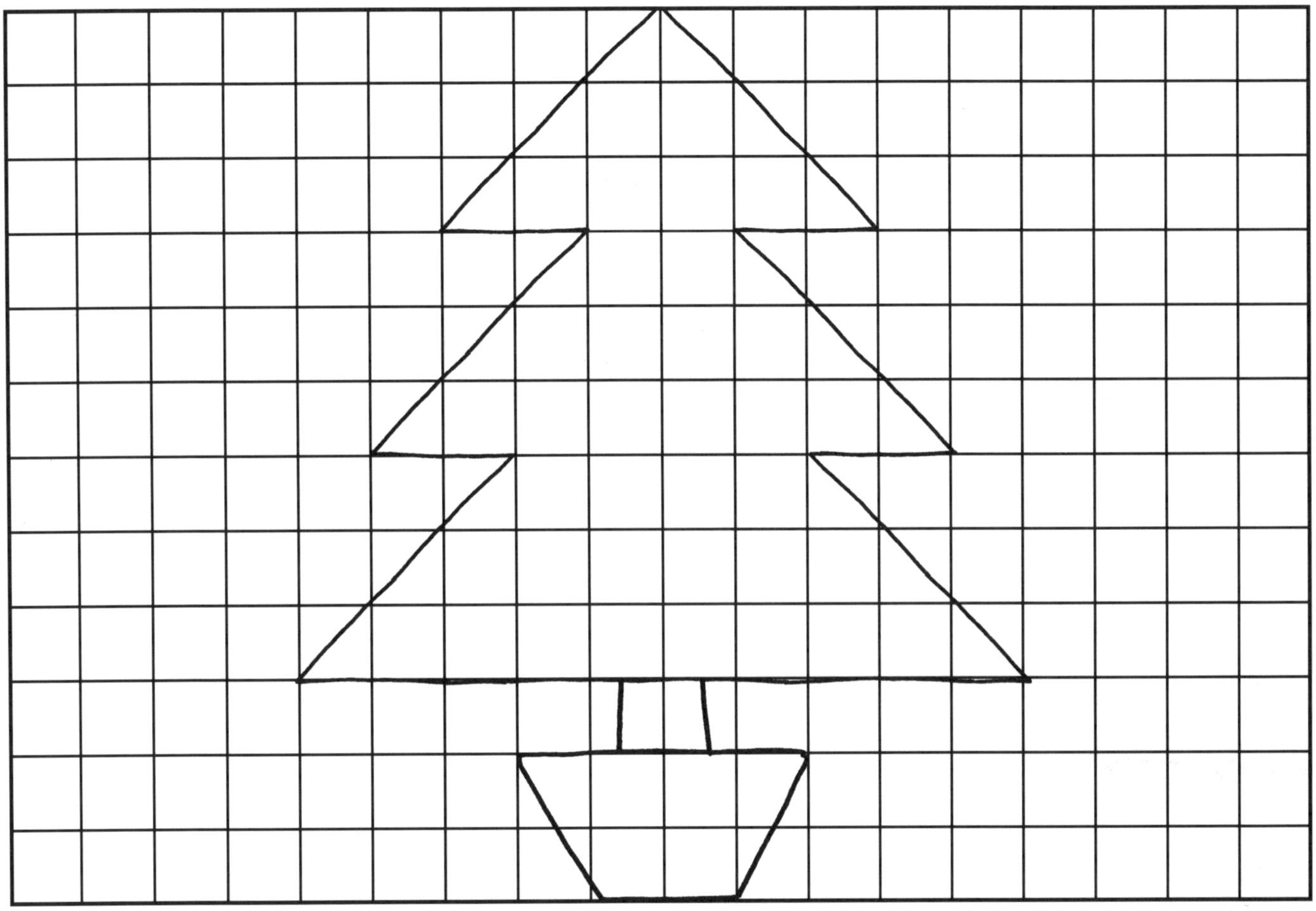

---

1. Estimate the area of the pot. ☐

2. Find the area of the pot. ☐

3. Estimate the area of the Christmas tree including its trunk. ☐

4. Find the area of the Christmas tree including its trunk. ☐

5. Colour the trunk of the tree brown, then colour the rest of the tree green.

6. Measure the perimeter of the pot, to the nearest millimetre. ☐

7. Measure the perimeter of the green part of the tree, to the nearest millimetre. ☐

Notes for teachers
Objective: Measure the perimeter and area of simple shapes
Most pupils will have found areas of shapes by counting squares during their numeracy work in Y4. The worksheets here provide revision of this work as well as introducing further work on perimeters, as recommended for Y5. Encourage the children to use the correct units of measurement i.e. square centimetres for area and centimetres for perimeter. The actual area of the pot is 6cm². The actual area of the tree is 45cm².

Andrew Brodie: Christmas Maths 9–11 © A & C Black Publishers Ltd. 2006   13

Taking measurements (2)

Name: Date:

Use the grid to draw your own Christmas picture. Don't make the picture too complicated because you have to find the area and perimeter of what you have drawn!

The area of my picture is ☐   The perimeter of my picture is ☐

Notes for teachers
Objective: Measure the perimeter and area of simple shapes
It is easier if pupils choose 'simple' shapes such as Christmas stockings, reindeer, Father Christmas, bells, etc.

Christmas coordinates

Name:  Date:

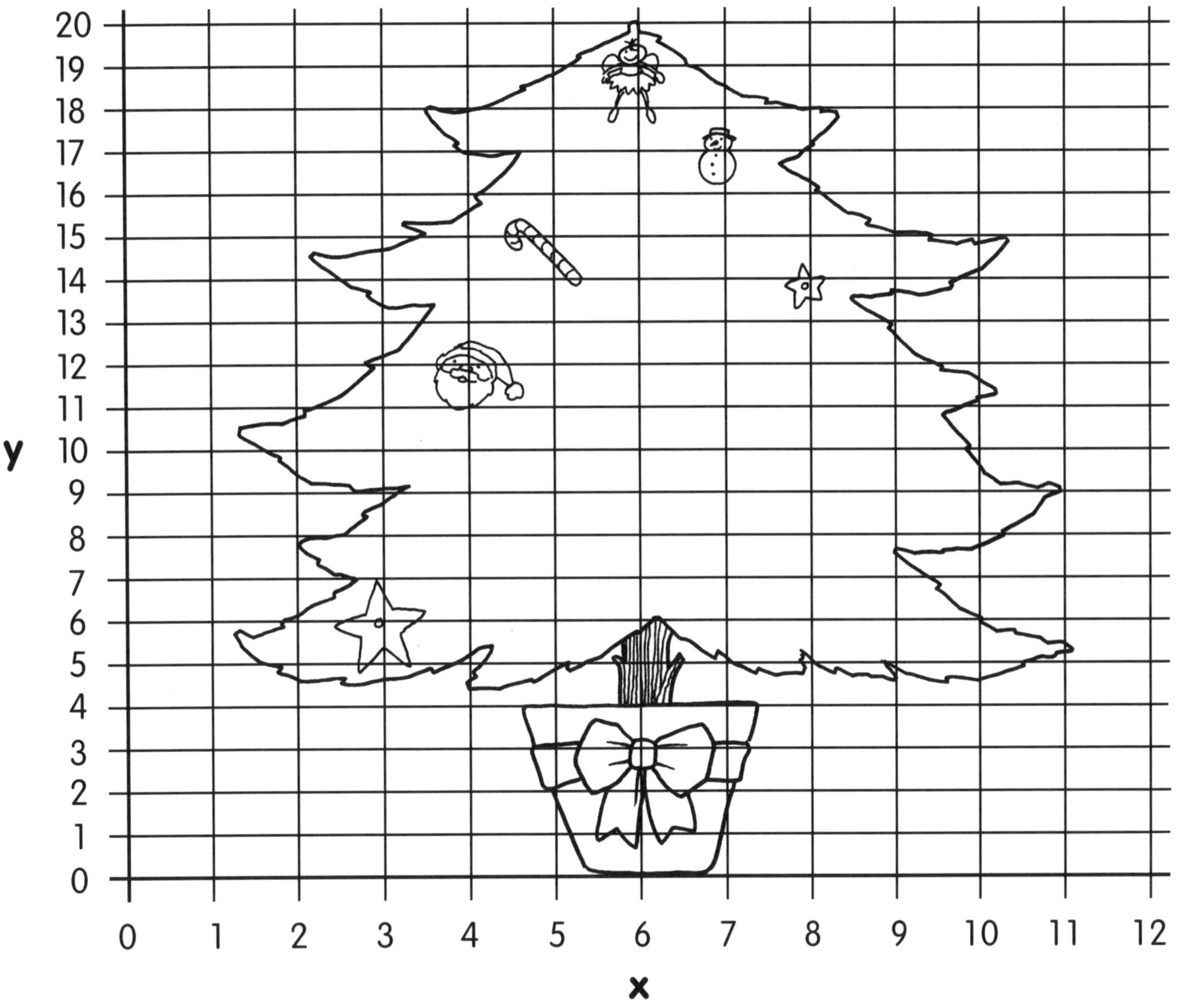

Use coordinates to identify the positions of the following:

The fairy is at ....

The small star is at ....

The big star is at ....

The candy cane is at ....

The snowman is at ....

Father Christmas is at ....

Draw some baubles on the tree and colour them all differently, then ask your friend to write down the coordinates of the baubles.

Notes for teachers
Objective: Read and plot coordinates in the first quadrant
See page 48 for correct answers.

A cold, cold Christmas (1)

Name:  Date:

Read the passage below and answer the question on Worksheet 14.

One special year it began to snow at 4pm on Christmas Eve when the temperature was approximately 0° Celsius. By 6pm the temperature had dropped to −2°C and it was still snowing. The snow carried on falling for about another hour but by 8pm all the clouds had gone and the night was clear so that the stars were visible. It was even colder then — the temperature had gone down by another three degrees. The temperature continued to fall until midnight when it got another two degrees colder, but then the sky became cloudy and the temperature began to rise.

At 7 o'clock on Christmas morning the snow was still thick on the ground but the temperature was four degrees higher than it had been at midnight. By 9am it had gone up to freezing point again. The clouds had cleared and the sun was shining brightly. People were enjoying the snow, building snowmen, playing on sledges and throwing snowballs. At 10am the sun was helping to melt the snow. The temperature was 2°C.

By noon the temperature had reached 4°C.

Notes for teachers
Objectives: Recognise and use negative numbers in the context of temperature; use vocabulary related to time. This sheet provides information in the form of temperatures and times to be used with Worksheet 14.

A cold, cold Christmas (2)

Name: Date:

Using the information from Worksheet 13, show the correct temperatures on these thermometers. Under each thermometer write the time using 24 hour clock notation.

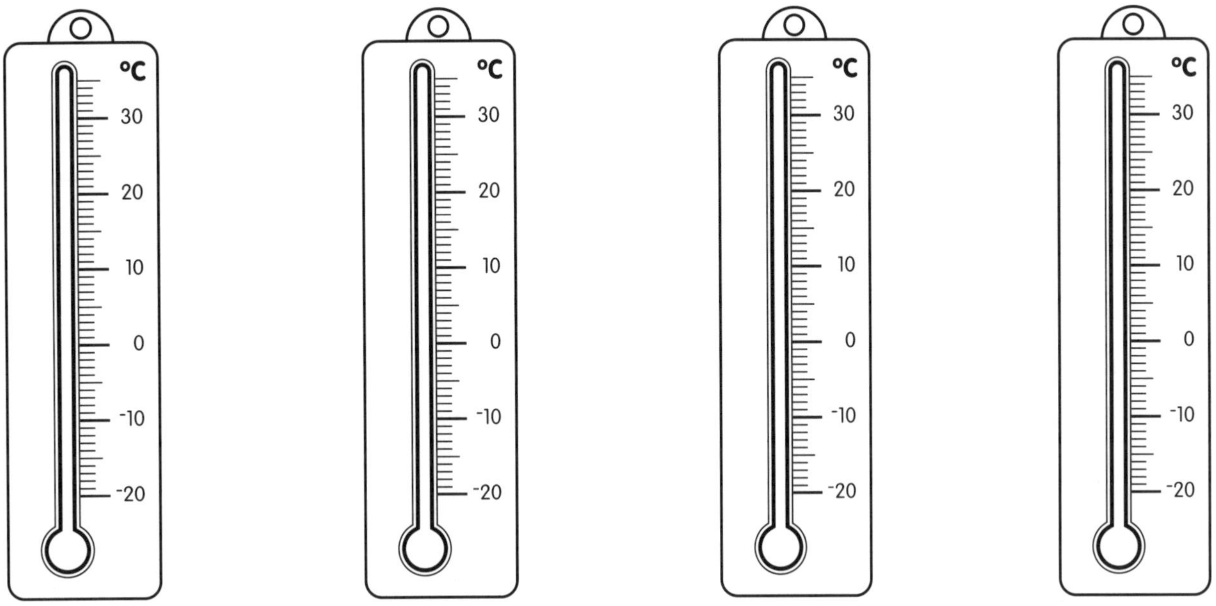

4 pm ☐   6 pm ☐   8 pm ☐   12 midnight ☐

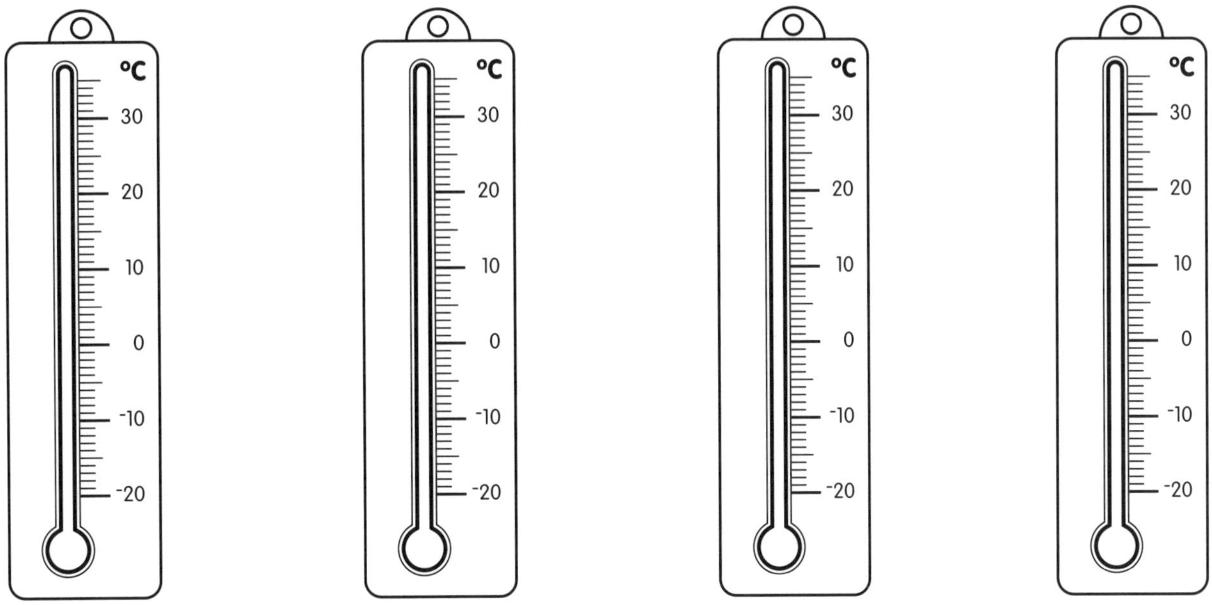

7 am ☐   9 am ☐   10 am ☐   12 noon ☐

Notes for teachers
Objective: Recognise and use negative numbers in the context of temperature; use vocabulary related to time.
See page 48 for correct answers.

Christmas multiples

Name: Date:

Look at these Christmas pictures.

Colour the robin red, the star yellow and the bauble green.

On the grid, draw and colour the following pictures:

Robins on the multiples of nine, stars on the multiples of four, baubles on the multiples of six. Don't draw them too big because some squares will have more than one picture.

1	2	3	4	5	6	7	8	9
10	11	12	13	14	15	16	17	18
19	20	21	22	23	24	25	26	27
28	29	30	31	32	33	34	35	36
37	38	39	40	41	42	43	44	45
46	47	48	49	50	51	52	53	54
55	56	57	58	59	60	61	62	63
64	65	66	67	68	69	70	71	72
73	74	75	76	77	78	79	80	81

Notes for teachers
Objective: Properties of number sequences
The children should extend beyond their tables knowledge when identifying the multiples of four or six, i.e. they should identify 44, 48, 52, 56, 60, 64, 68, 72, 76 and 80 as multiples of four. Once the pupils have completed the task, ask them which numbers are multiples of both four and six, or four and nine, or six and nine, or four, six and nine.

Christmas Town

Name: Date:

Santa will need to deliver gifts to the good people of Christmas Town. The houses in Christmas Town are numbered rather strangely. In each street the house numbers follow a special sequence. Unfortunately the numbers are missing from some of the front doors.

Put the correct number on the door of each house.

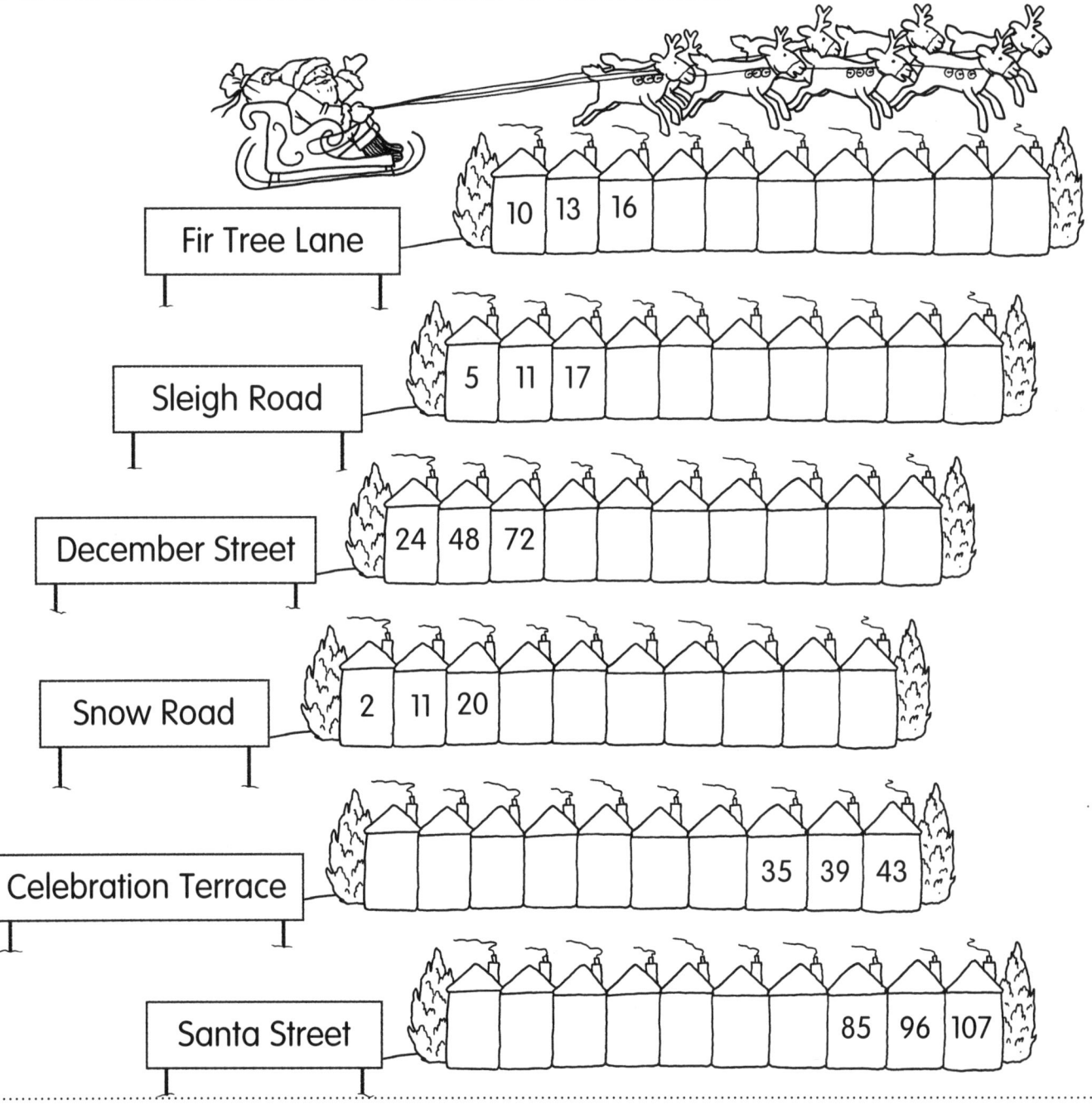

Fir Tree Lane: 10 13 16

Sleigh Road: 5 11 17

December Street: 24 48 72

Snow Road: 2 11 20

Celebration Terrace: 35 39 43

Santa Street: 85 96 107

Notes for teachers
Objective: Properties of number sequences
An extension to this activity would be for children to imagine each street to have had another ten houses and to continue the sequence to include these – the extra houses could be 5 on either end of the street hence including negative numbers. See page 48 for correct answers.

Worksheet 17 — Match the presents

Name:  Date:

Each child has an improper fraction written on their clothes.
Each parcel has a mixed number on it.

Match the numbers to find out which child will receive each present.
Write the correct name on each gift tag.

The first one has been done for you.

Children with fractions:
- Zac $\frac{7}{4}$
- Kai $\frac{6}{4}$
- Lea $\frac{27}{5}$
- Ellie $\frac{13}{2}$
- Eve $\frac{41}{10}$
- Jack $\frac{11}{8}$
- Toru $\frac{5}{2}$
- Mel $\frac{19}{5}$
- Sita $\frac{12}{3}$
- Abe $\frac{12}{4}$

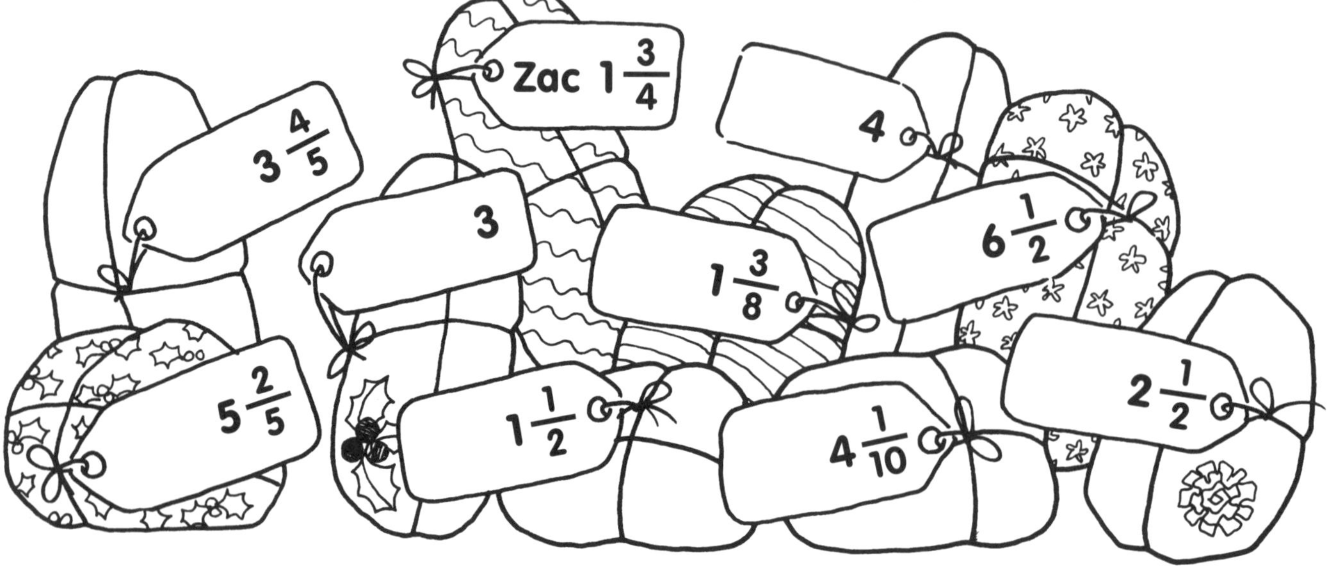

Gift tags:
- Zac $1\frac{3}{4}$
- $3\frac{4}{5}$
- 3
- 4
- $1\frac{3}{8}$
- $6\frac{1}{2}$
- $5\frac{2}{5}$
- $1\frac{1}{2}$
- $4\frac{1}{10}$
- $2\frac{1}{2}$

Notes for teachers
Objective: Change an improper fraction to a mixed number
Ensure pupils have a clear understanding of the terms 'mixed number' and 'improper fraction'. Answers on page 48.

20   Andrew Brodie: Christmas Maths 9–11 © A & C Black Publishers Ltd. 2006

Feeding the reindeer

Name: Date:

The Christmas deliveries have been done and the reindeer are hungry. Match the equivalent fractions to find out which feed box belongs to each of the reindeer.

Write the correct reindeer's name on each feed box.
The first one has been done for you.

Reindeer with fractions:
- Vixen $\frac{18}{20}$
- Rudolph $\frac{2}{6}$
- Dancer $\frac{8}{10}$
- Prancer $\frac{2}{3}$
- Blitzen $\frac{2}{7}$
- Cupid $\frac{70}{100}$
- Comet $\frac{1}{2}$
- Donner $\frac{18}{30}$
- Dasher $\frac{3}{4}$

Feed boxes:
- $\frac{1}{3}$
- $\frac{4}{6}$
- Vixen $\frac{9}{10}$
- $\frac{9}{15}$
- $\frac{6}{8}$
- $\frac{5}{10}$
- $\frac{4}{14}$
- $\frac{4}{5}$
- $\frac{7}{10}$

Notes for teachers
Objective: Recognise when two simple fractions are equivalent
An extension to this activity would be to ask pupils to write another fraction that is equivalent to each pair given.
Answers on page 48.

Andrew Brodie: Christmas Maths 9–11 © A & C Black Publishers Ltd. 2006

Cooking the turkey (1)

Name:  Date:

To cook a turkey properly you should put it in the oven for approximately forty minutes per kilogram. The turkey in the picture weighed five kilograms before it was cooked.

1. For how many minutes should the turkey be cooked?

2. How many hours and minutes is this?

3. If the family want the turkey to be cooked by 1.30 pm, at what time should they put it in the oven?

4. If the family want the turkey to be cooked by 1.00 pm, at what time should they put it in the oven?

5. If the family want the turkey to be cooked by 2.15 pm, at what time should they put it in the oven?

Notes for teachers
Objective: Solve simple problems involving ratio
Answers on page 48.

Cooking the turkey (2)

Name: Date:

To cook a turkey properly you should put it in the oven for approximately forty minutes per kilogram.

The chart below shows cooking times for different turkeys. Some of the chart has been completed. Write the appropriate information to complete the chart.

Weight of turkey (out of the oven)	Cooking time (minutes)	Cooking time (hours and minutes)	Time in the oven	Time out of the oven
4 kg			10 am	
4.5 kg			10 am	
5 kg			10.30 am	
5.5 kg			9.45 am	
6 kg				1.30 pm
6.5 kg				2 pm
7 kg			9.30 am	
7.5 kg				2 pm
8 kg				2.15 pm
8.5 kg			8 am	
9 kg			7.30 am	
9.5 kg				2 pm
10 kg				2 pm

Notes for teachers
Objective: Solve simple problems involving ratio
See page 48 for the completed chart.

Counting the days (1)

Name:  Date:

December

....	....	....	....	....	....	....

Complete this page from a calendar by writing in the days of the week and the dates as they should appear on this year's calendar. Use your best handwriting and don't forget that the name of every day starts with a capital letter.

Notes for teachers
Objective: Understand time on calendars; spell days of the week.
Pupils can consider this to be their personal advent calendar showing the whole month of December.

24   Andrew Brodie: Christmas Maths 9–11 © A & C Black Publishers Ltd. 2006

Counting the days (2)

Name: Date:

Use the calendar page from Worksheet 21 to help you to answer these questions.

1. On which day of the week is Christmas Day this year?

   ----

2. On which day of the week is Christmas Eve this year?

   ----

3. On which day of the week is Boxing Day this year?

   ----

4. On which day of the week is New Year's Eve this year?

   ----

5. What is the day and date exactly two weeks before Christmas Day?

   ----

6. What is the day and date two weeks and four days before Christmas Day?

   ----

7. What is the day and date one week and two days before Christmas Day?

   ----

8. What is the day and date six days before Christmas Day?

   ----

9. What is the day and date five days after Christmas Day?

   ----

10. What is the day and date one week after Christmas Day?

Notes for teachers
Objective: Understand time on calendars; spell days of the week.
Christmas Day provides an ideal 'target' for pupils' calculations regarding the counting of time in weeks and days. They should be encouraged to consider time differences by 'jumping' from one date to another – so, for example, they can jump back two weeks from Christmas, then make three jumps back to find the day and date two weeks and three days before Christmas Day.

Andrew Brodie: Christmas Maths 9–11 © A & C Black Publishers Ltd. 2006   25

Christmas visitors (1)

Name:  Date:

Read the poem below and answer the questions on Worksheet 24.

'Twas the night before Christmas at the Snow View Hotel,
Preparations for lunch time were going quite well.
The chef in the kitchen was working with care,
Ready for all the guests that would be there.
While people were sleeping all snug in their beds,
The chef worked, his tall white hat perched on his head.

Six turkeys with stuffing all ready to roast,
Ten saucepans of fresh soup, and croutons to toast.
Eight strings of sausages (fifteen in each string).
Sprouts, carrots and green beans all fit for a king.
Twelve litres of gravy, and then four of sauce,
A small pinch of salt, and some pepper of course.

Eight Christmas puds made with four kilos of fruit,
Six cakes topped with robins all looking so cute.
With the puddings came custard or ice cream to eat,
Followed by mince pies, or cake very sweet.
Finally coffee, with chocolates to munch,
Just one chocolate each to finish this lunch.

The work was eventually finished that night.
In the kitchen, chef finally turned out the light.
'It's bed time' he thought to himself as he yawned,
And fell fast asleep as Christmas day dawned.
Later that day, all the guests ate their dinner
And enjoyed every mouthful (and no one got thinner!).

£12.75 each

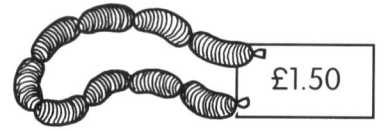
£1.50

£3.60 per kilo

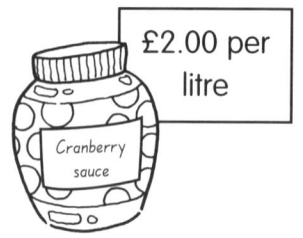
£2.00 per litre

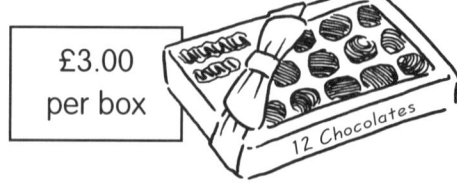
£3.00 per box

17p each

Notes for teachers
Objective: Solve problems involving money and measures
This sheet provides an excellent opportunity for careful reading. The information that the sheet contains, both within the poem and around the edges, will be needed by the pupils when completing Worksheets 24 to 26.

Christmas visitors (2)

Name:  Date:

60 guests were expected for Christmas dinner at the Snow View Hotel, so the chef had prepared enough for all of them.

Complete the table below to show the costs for some of the food items needed for all 60 guests.

Food	Calculation	Total Cost
Turkeys		
Strings of sausages		
Mixed Fruit		
Cranberry Sauce		
Chocolates		

1. What was the total cost of all these ingredients?

2. What was the mean average cost per guest, to the nearest whole pound?

Calculation space

Notes for teachers
Objective: Solve problems involving money and measures
Answers on page 48.

Andrew Brodie: Christmas Maths 9–11 © A & C Black Publishers Ltd. 2006   27

Christmas visitors (3)

Name:  Date:

Look again at the poem on Worksheet 23 and at your calculations on Worksheet 24.

If all the ingredients had been reduced in price by 10% what would the total prices have been?

Food	Total cost	10%	Cost reduced by 10%
Turkeys			
Strings of sausages			
Mixed Fruit			
Cranberry Sauce			
Chocolates			

1. What was the total reduced cost of all these ingredients?

2. Has the mean average cost per guest, to the nearest whole pound, changed?

Calculation space

Notes for teachers
Objective: Solve problems involving money and measures
Remind the pupils they can complete the second column of the table simply by copying the total costs from Worksheet 24. Answers on page 48.

28　Andrew Brodie: Christmas Maths 9–11 © A & C Black Publishers Ltd. 2006

Christmas visitors (4)

Name:  Date:

To complete this page you will need to remember some key facts:

How many grams are there in one kilogram? [ ]

How many millilitres are there in one litre? [ ]

Check that your answers to the above questions are correct before you complete the table below.

Complete the table below to show how much of each item is needed for one person and for 60 people. Some parts of the table have been completed for you. Use appropriate units of measurement to record your results. You will need to refer to Worksheet 23.

Item	1 person	60 people
Turkey	$\frac{1}{10}$ of a turkey	6 turkeys
Ice – cream	200ml	
Custard		12 litres
Soup (saucepans full)		10
Croutons	50g	
Sausages		120
Sprouts	6	
Green Beans		$7\frac{1}{2}$ kilos
Carrots		$7\frac{1}{2}$ kilos
Mince Pies	1	

Calculation space

Notes for teachers
Objective: Solve problems involving money and measures
The children should make good use of the calculation space to work out the amounts required in each cell. See page 48 for answers.

Christmas visitors (5)

Name:  Date:

Each guest paid £22.50 for their lunch. They had a delicious meal complete with Christmas crackers and party hats!

Calculate the total cost for:

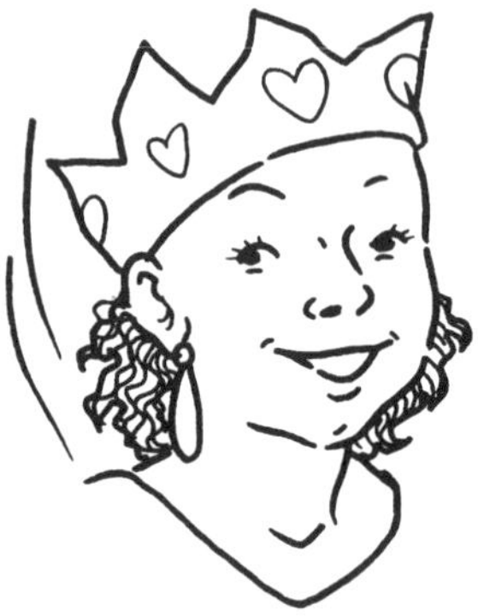

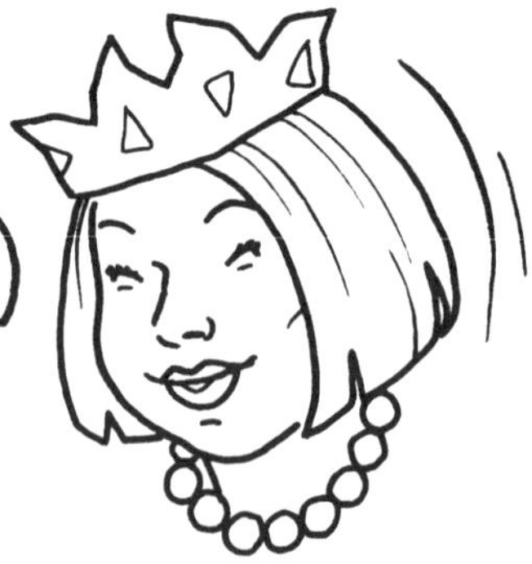

2 people ....

5 people ....

7 people ....

10 people ....

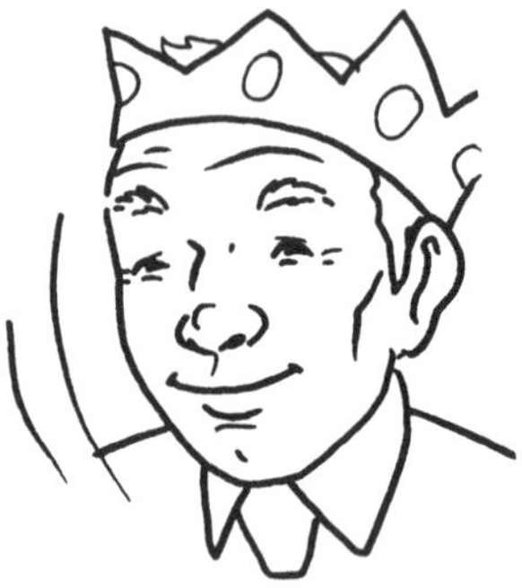

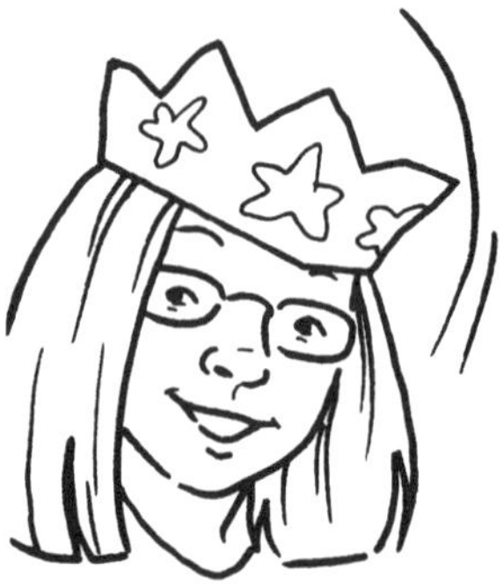

12 people ....

16 people ....

20 people ....

25 people ....

50 people ....

60 people ....

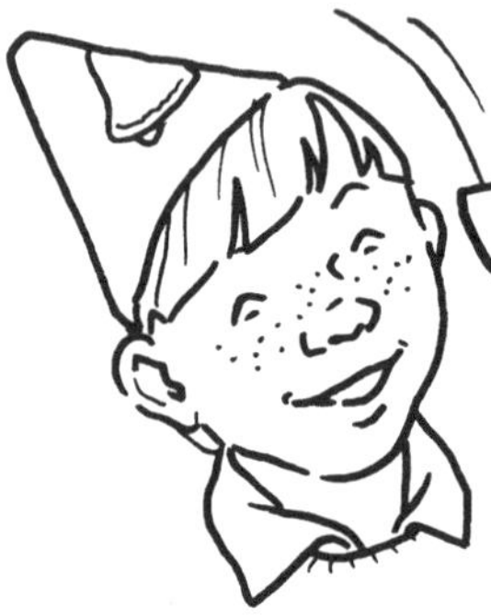

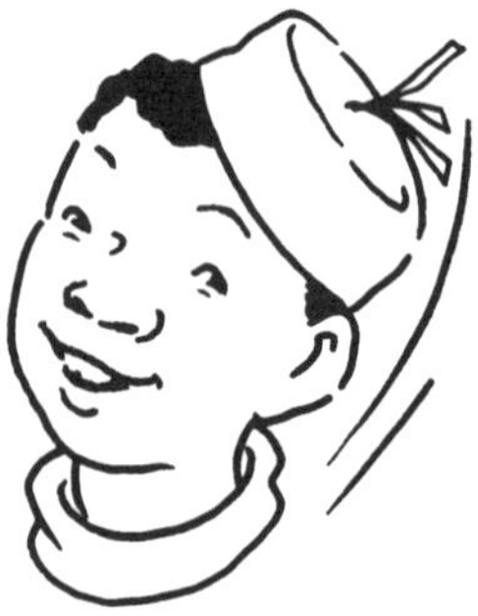

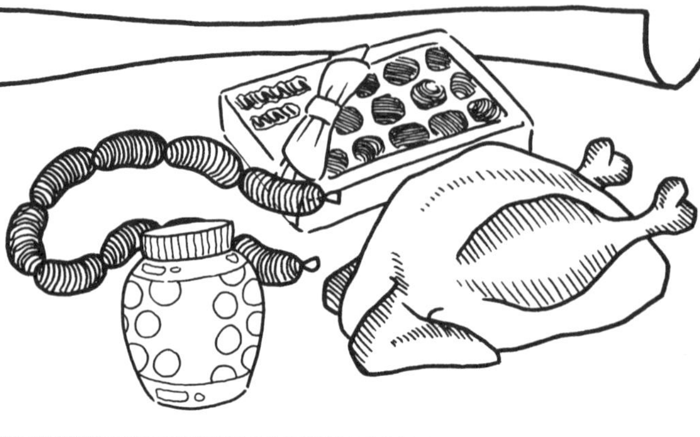

Notes for teachers
Objective: Solve problems involving money and measures
Answers on page 48. An extension activity for this final page of the set would be to ask pupils to make up questions for other pupils to answer (after of course working out the answers themselves). Alternatively, you could add in some questions about timings. These could possibly involve either guests' travelling times to the hotel from various destinations, or cooking times of some of the dinner items.

Santa's workshop (1)

Name:  Date:

In the months leading up to Christmas, Santa's workshop was alive with the sounds of humming, buzzing, drilling and sawing. The table shows how many toys were made each month from June to November.

Use the information on the table to answer the questions below.

Toys	June	July	August	September	October	November
Bicycles	16	26	31	20	22	17
Dolls	20	20	22	18	20	20
Board games	28	18	20	25	21	14
Footballs	25	23	27	21	22	20
Skateboards	10	17	15	19	12	11
Totals						

Complete the statements:

1. A total of .... bicycles were made.
2. A total of .... dolls were made.
3. A total of .... board games were made.
4. A total of .... footballs were made.
5. A total of .... skateboards were made.
6. In June a total of .... toys were made.
7. In July a total of .... toys were made.
8. In August a total of .... toys were made.
9. In September a total of .... toys were made.
10. In October a total of .... toys were made.
11. In November a total of .... toys were made.
12. During the six months a grand total of .... toys were made.

Notes for teachers
Objective: Begin to find the mean of a set of data
Encourage pupils to check this in both directions on the chart: ie, both sets of data should add up to 600. This sheet should be used in conjunction with Worksheet 29. Answers on page 48.

Andrew Brodie: Christmas Maths 9–11 © A & C Black Publishers Ltd. 2006   31

Santa's workshop (2)

Name:  Date:

Look again at the data on Worksheet 28.

Calculate the 'mean' number of each type of toy made each month by adding the numbers made each month and dividing the total by the number of months.

The first one has been done for you.

Toys	Total made	Calculation needed	Mean
Bicycles	132	132 ÷ 6	22
Dolls			
Board games			
Footballs			
Skateboards			

Santa needed 150 of each toy by Christmas – how many more of each toy must be made?

☐ more bicycles

☐ more dolls

☐ more board games

☐ more skateboards

☐ more footballs

Calculation space

Notes for teachers
Objective: Begin to find the mean of a set of data
You may need to show some children that there are less extra board games needed than dolls because more board games than dolls have already been made – a common mistake made by children occurs when subtracting numbers such as 126 from 150; many pupils are likely to write 34 as the answer. This can be overcome by encouraging them to 'count on' from 126 to 130 and then to 150. Answers on page 48. Pupils could be asked to make up some more questions for a friend to work out. These might include creating a line graph for one of more of the toys, or calculating the ranges of numbers of toys made.

32   Andrew Brodie: Christmas Maths 9–11 © A & C Black Publishers Ltd. 2006

Oh Christmas tree!

Worksheet 30

Name: Date:

Answer the questions about the trees.

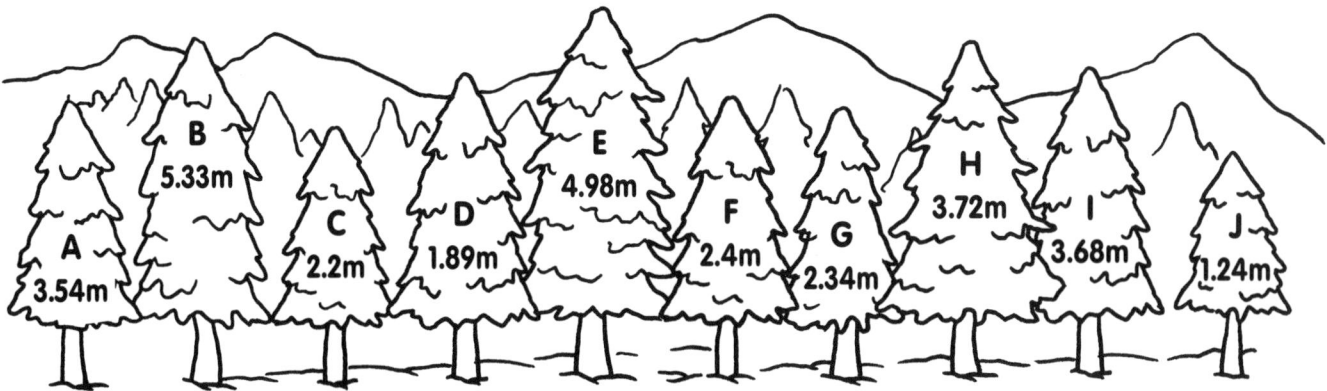

1. Calculate the difference between the heights of the following pairs of trees. Give your answer in metres.

Trees A and B ☐   Trees A and I ☐   Trees J and B ☐

Trees D and E ☐   Trees F and C ☐   Trees C and D ☐

Trees E and F ☐   Trees B and C ☐   Trees G and H ☐

Trees I and J ☐   Trees F and G ☐   Trees D and H ☐

2. Calculate the total height of trees A, B and C. ☐

3. Calculate the total height of trees C, D and E. ☐

4. Calculate the total height of trees D, H and J. ☐

5. The trees grow 4 centimetres each month.

Calculate the height of each tree after one more year.

Tree A ☐   Tree B ☐   Tree C ☐   Tree D ☐   Tree E ☐

Tree F ☐   Tree G ☐   Tree H ☐   Tree I ☐   Tree J ☐

Notes for teachers
Objective: Find differences by counting up; use informal pencil and paper methods to record additions and subtractions. Encourage pupils to count on from the shorter tree to the taller tree in each pair. Answers on page 48.

Andrew Brodie: Christmas Maths 9–11 © A & C Black Publishers Ltd. 2006

Complete the puzzle (1)

Name:

 Date:

Cut out the square puzzle pieces. Each one has a number on it.

The answer to each of the calculations on Worksheet 32 will show you where to stick the pieces to complete the picture.

Notes for teachers
Objective: Understand percentage as the number of parts per hundred and find simple percentages of numbers
This worksheet needs to be used in conjunction with Worksheet 32. Before beginning this activity, remind pupils that 50% = half, 25% = a quarter, etc.

34 Andrew Brodie: Christmas Maths 9–11 © A & C Black Publishers Ltd. 2006

Complete the puzzle (2)

Name: Date:

10% of 50	10% of 100	10% of 260	10% of 500	10% of 70
10% of 90	10% of 130	25% of 100	25% of 32	25% of 60
25% of 12	25% of 80	25% of 1000	25% of 300	20% of 500
20% of 200	20% of 30	20% of 60	20% of 90	20% of 120
30% of 100	30% of 200	30% of 150	75% of 100	75% of 300
75% of 36	75% of 1000	50% of 46	50% of 44	50% of 88
50% of 34	50% of 42	1% of 100	1% of 50	1% of 200

Notes for teachers
Objective: Understand percentage as the number of parts per hundred and find simple percentages of numbers
An extension to this activity could be for pupils to use Christmas pictures (perhaps old Christmas cards) to create their own puzzle pictures for other pupils to complete.

Andrew Brodie: Christmas Maths 9–11 © A & C Black Publishers Ltd. 2006   35

Worksheet 33: The twelve days of Christmas (1)

Name:  Date:

How many presents do you get for Christmas?

Read this rhyme and answer the questions on Worksheet 35.

On the first day of Christmas
My true love gave to me
A partridge in a pear tree.

On the second day of Christmas
My true love gave to me
Two turtle doves and
A partridge in a pear tree.

On the third day of Christmas
My true love gave to me
Three French hens,
Two turtle doves and
A partridge in a pear tree.

On the fourth day of Christmas
My true love gave to me
Four calling birds,
Three French hens,
Two turtle doves and
A partridge in a pear tree.

On the fifth day of Christmas
My true love gave to me
Five gold rings,
Four calling birds,
Three French hens,
Two turtle doves and
A partridge in a pear tree.

On the sixth day of Christmas
My true love gave to me
Six geese a-laying,
Five gold rings,
Four calling birds,
Three French hens,
Two turtle doves and
A partridge in a pear tree.

On the seventh day of Christmas
My true love gave to me
Seven swans a-swimming,
Six geese a-laying,
Five gold rings,
Four calling birds,
Three French hens,
Two turtle doves and
A partridge in a pear tree.

On the eighth day of Christmas
My true love gave to me
Eight maids a-milking,
Seven swans a-swimming,
Six geese a-laying,
Five gold rings,
Four calling birds,
Three French hens,
Two turtle doves and
A partridge in a pear tree.

Notes for teachers
Objectives: 'Using and applying' mathematical skills; properties of numbers and number sequences; calculation strategies, both mental and written; solve problems.
This famous Christmas song provides lots of opportunities for fun and meaningful maths work. Children should be encouraged to see the humour in the song: Who on earth would buy this range of presents for someone they loved? Where would the presents be kept? Exactly how many presents were there?

The twelve days of Christmas (2)

Name: Date:

On the ninth day of Christmas
My true love gave to me
Nine ladies dancing,
Eight maids a-milking,
Seven swans a-swimming,
Six geese a-laying,
Five gold rings,
Four calling birds,
Three French hens,
Two turtle doves and
A partridge in a pear tree.

On the tenth day of Christmas
My true love gave to me
Ten lords a-leaping,
Nine ladies dancing,
Eight maids a-milking,
Seven swans a-swimming,
Six geese a-laying,
Five gold rings,
Four calling birds,
Three French hens,
Two turtle doves and
A partridge in a pear tree.

On the eleventh day of Christmas
My true love gave to me
Eleven pipers piping,
Ten lords a-leaping,
Nine ladies dancing,
Eight maids a-milking,
Seven swans a-swimming,
Six geese a-laying,
Five gold rings,
Four calling birds,
Three French hens,
Two turtle doves and
A partridge in a pear tree.

On the twelfth day of Christmas
My true love gave to me
Twelve drummers drumming,
Eleven pipers piping,
Ten lords a-leaping,
Nine ladies dancing,
Eight maids a-milking,
Seven swans a-swimming,
Six geese a-laying,
Five gold rings,
Four calling birds,
Three French hens,
Two turtle doves and
A partridge in a pear tree.

Notes for teachers
Objective: 'Using and applying' mathematical skills; properties of numbers and number sequences; calculation strategies, both mental and written; solve problems.
The pupils may also enjoy rewriting the song, giving it modern words:
On the first day of Christmas
My true love gave to me
A game for my computer…

Worksheet 35

The twelve days of Christmas (3)

Name: Date:

You will need Worksheets 33 and 34 to answer these questions. Complete the chart below showing all the presents given. We have started it for you.

Presents		Total
Partridge	1 + 1 + 1 + 1 + 1 + 1 + 1 + 1 + 1 + 1 + 1 + 1	12
Turtle doves		
French hens		
Calling birds		
Gold rings		
Geese		
Swans		
Maids		
Ladies		
Lords		
Pipers		
Drummers		

Which was the present that the true love gave the most of? _____

Notes for teachers
Objective: 'Using and applying' mathematical skills; properties of numbers and number sequences; calculation strategies, both mental and written; solve problems.
In addition to the questions on this sheet, ask the pupils how many presents were given each day: can they see the sequence developing? You may like to ask the pupils to represent each present by a dot: on the first day there was one dot; on the second day there were two dots plus one dot; on the third day there were three dots, then two dots, then one dot:
The pattern will reveal the sequence of triangular numbers 1, 3, 6, 10, 15, 21, etc. As well as these questions, encourage pupils to invent their own questions to investigate.

38   Andrew Brodie: Christmas Maths 9–11 © A & C Black Publishers Ltd. 2006

Worksheet 36

Treats for Santa (1)

Name: Date:

On Christmas Eve many homes leave out a drink for Santa Claus and a carrot for his reindeer. Look at what has been left out in the homes below.

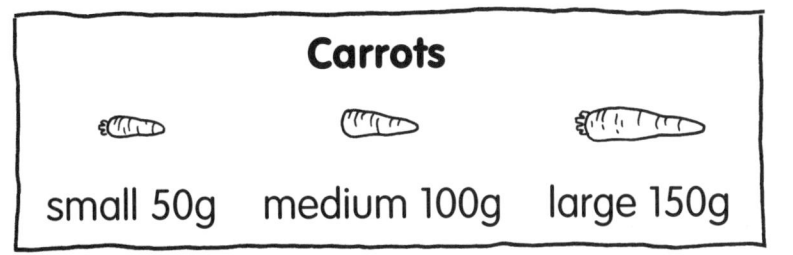

Carrots
small 50g   medium 100g   large 150g

Beer 250ml   **Juice** 125ml   **Sherry** 50ml

Festive Street: 1, 2, 3, 4, 5

Frosty Road: 1, 2, 3, 4, 5

Starlight Lane: 1, 2, 3, 4, 5

Winter Avenue: 1, 2, 3, 4, 5

Now answer the questions on Worksheets 37 and 38.

Notes for teachers
Objective: Use, read and write standard metric measures; solve problems including 'real life' money or measures. The information given on this worksheet will be needed to answer the questions on Worksheets 37 and 38.

Andrew Brodie: Christmas Maths 9–11 © A & C Black Publishers Ltd. 2006

Worksheet 37: Treats for Santa (2)

Name:
Date:

Answer the questions below.

1. What was the total volume of drink left out in:

   a) Festive Street? ☐
   b) Frosty Road? ☐
   c) Starlight Lane? ☐
   d) Winter Avenue? ☐

2. What volume of drink was left out in total? ☐

3. How much beer was left out? ☐

4. How much juice was left out? ☐

5. How much Sherry was left out? ☐

Beer costs £2.20 per litre   Juice costs £1.44 per litre
Sherry costs £10.00 per litre

6. With this information calculate the following. (Remember to show your working out.)

   Cost of drinks on Festive Street ☐

   Cost of drinks on Frosty Road ☐

   Cost of drinks on Starlight Lane ☐

   Total cost of all the beer ☐

   Total cost of all the sherry ☐

   Total cost of all the juice ☐

   Total spent on all the drinks ☐

Notes for teachers
Objective: Use, read and write standard metric measures; solve problems including 'real life' money or measures. As an extension activity, you could allocate amounts of time for Santa to deliver each home their presents and to drink each type of drink. Pupils could then calculate how long various deliveries would take. See page 48 for correct answers.

Andrew Brodie: Christmas Maths 9–11 © A & C Black Publishers Ltd. 2006

worksheet 38

Treats for Santa (3)

Name: Date:

Carrots cost £1 per kilo. Calculate the cost of drink and carrots left at each house. Record your answers in the spaces indicated below.

No.1 Festive Street	☐	No.4 Festive Street	☐
No.2 Festive Street	☐	No.5 Festive Street	☐
No.3 Festive Street	☐	Total for the whole street	☐

No.1 Frosty Road	☐	No.4 Frosty Road	☐
No.2 Frosty Road	☐	No.5 Frosty Road	☐
No.3 Frosty Road	☐	Total for the whole street	☐

No.1 Starlight Lane	☐	No.4 Starlight Lane	☐
No.2 Starlight Lane	☐	No.5 Starlight Lane	☐
No.3 Starlight Lane	☐	Total for the whole street	☐

No.1 Winter Avenue	☐	No.4 Winter Avenue	☐
No.2 Winter Avenue	☐	No.5 Winter Avenue	☐
No.3 Winter Avenue	☐	Total for the whole street	☐

Grand total cost for drink and carrots for all 20 houses ☐

Notes for teachers
Objective: Use, read and write standard metric measures; solve problems including 'real life' money or measures. An extension to this activity could be to make a reduction of 10% off the prices of carrots and drinks and to re-calculate the prices.

Andrew Brodie: Christmas Maths 9–11 © A & C Black Publishers Ltd. 2006

Worksheet 39: Chocolate decorations

Name: Date:

The tree decorations can be bought individually or they can be bought in packs of ten of any one type.

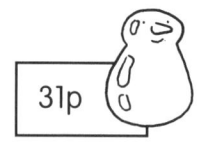

27p   31p   34p

1. What would be the price of a pack of ten snowmen?
2. What would be the price of a pack of ten bells?
3. What would be the price of a pack of ten Santas?

Ten packs are packed in a box.

4. What would be the price of a box of bells?
5. What would be the price of a box of snowmen?
6. What would be the price of a box of Santas?

One hundred boxes are packed in a container.

7. What would be the price of a container of Santas?
8. What would be the price of a container of bells?
9. What would be the price of a container of snowmen?

A chain of supermarkets orders 1 container of bells, 3 containers of Santas and 2 containers of snowmen.

10. What is the value of all these decorations?

Because the supermarket company is buying so many decorations they are given a 70% discount.

11. How much is the discount worth and how much do they actually pay?

a) Discount

b) Actual cost to the company

Notes for teachers
Objective: Multiply whole numbers by 10, 100; use multiplication to solve word problems involving money. The pupils should show their answers with correct notation, using a pound sign and no 'p'. Answers on page 48.

Christmas stars

Name: Date:

x	1	2	3	4	5	6	7	8	9	10
1	1	2	3	4	5	6	7	8	9	10
2	2	4	6	8	10	12	14	16	18	20
3	3	6	9	12	15	18	21	24	27	30
4	4	8	12	16	20	24	28	32	36	40
5	5	10	15	20	25	30	35	40	45	50
6	6	12	18	24	30	36	42	48	54	60
7	7	14	21	28	35	42	49	56	63	70
8	8	16	24	32	40	48	56	64	72	80
9	9	18	27	36	45	54	63	72	81	90
10	10	20	30	40	50	60	70	80	90	100

x	1	2	3	4	5	6	7	8	9	10
1	1	2	3	4	5	6	7	8	9	10
2	2	4	6	8	10	12	14	16	18	20
3	3	6	9	12	15	18	21	24	27	30
4	4	8	12	16	20	24	28	32	36	40
5	5	10	15	20	25	30	35	40	45	50
6	6	12	18	24	30	36	42	48	54	60
7	7	14	21	28	35	42	49	56	63	70
8	8	16	24	32	40	48	56	64	72	80
9	9	18	27	36	45	54	63	72	81	90
10	10	20	30	40	50	60	70	80	90	100

Notes for teachers
Objective: Recognise number sequences and patterns
To give this activity a Christmas theme, ask the children to draw stars in the squares as follows: multiples of two, multiples of three, multiples of four (make sure they include all multiples of four: i.e. where 2 x 6 gives 12, etc.), multiples of five, square numbers, etc. You may need to give each child several copies of this sheet but it is worth it to enable them to see the patterns created. Alternatively you could ask different groups of children to find different patterns then discuss what everyone has found in a plenary. For the results to be clear only one pattern should be created per multiplication square.

Andrew Brodie: Christmas Maths 9–11 © A & C Black Publishers Ltd. 2006

Worksheet 41: The 25th of December

Name:	Date:

The number 25 is quite special. It is a square number, for example.

1. What is the square root of 25? ☐

2. Two other square numbers add up to 25. What are they? ☐ ☐

3. Can you calculate the square of 25? ☐

4. 25 has only three factors. What are they? ☐ ☐ ☐

5. Do you know your 25 times table? It's a very useful multiplication table. Continue the one that is started for you, up to 10 x 25:

   1 x 25 = 25   ☐ ☐ ☐ ☐
   ☐ ☐ ☐ ☐ ☐

6. Look at the number 799 – its digits add up to 25. In which other three-digit numbers do the digits add up to 25?

   ☐ ☐ ☐ ☐ ☐

7. 25 can be made by adding other numbers together. Using only prime numbers find how many ways you can make 25. Use each prime number only once in any answer.

   ☐ ☐ ☐
   ☐ ☐

Notes for teachers
Objective: Solve mathematical problems; recognise and explain patterns and relationships.
This varied sheet includes some opportunities for investigations. See answers on page 48.

Worksheet 42

2007 Calendar

Name:　　　　　　　　　　　　　　　　　　　Date:

JANUARY
S	M	T	W	T	F	S
	1	2	3	4	5	6
7	8	9	10	11	12	13
14	15	16	17	18	19	20
21	22	23	24	25	26	27
28	29	30	31			

FEBRUARY
S	M	T	W	T	F	S
				1	2	3
4	5	6	7	8	9	10
11	12	13	14	15	16	17
18	19	20	21	22	23	24
25	26	27	28			

MARCH
S	M	T	W	T	F	S
				1	2	3
4	5	6	7	8	9	10
11	12	13	14	15	16	17
18	19	20	21	22	23	24
25	26	27	28	29	30	31

APRIL
S	M	T	W	T	F	S
1	2	3	4	5	6	7
8	9	10	11	12	13	14
15	16	17	18	19	20	21
22	23	24	25	26	27	28
29	30					

MAY
S	M	T	W	T	F	S
		1	2	3	4	5
6	7	8	9	10	11	12
13	14	15	16	17	18	19
20	21	22	23	24	25	26
27	28	29	30	31		

JUNE
S	M	T	W	T	F	S
					1	2
3	4	5	6	7	8	9
10	11	12	13	14	15	16
17	18	19	20	21	22	23
24	25	26	27	28	29	30

JULY
S	M	T	W	T	F	S
1	2	3	4	5	6	7
8	9	10	11	12	13	14
15	16	17	18	19	20	21
22	23	24	25	26	27	28
29	30	31				

AUGUST
S	M	T	W	T	F	S
			1	2	3	4
5	6	7	8	9	10	11
12	13	14	15	16	17	18
19	20	21	22	23	24	25
26	27	28	29	30	31	

SEPTEMBER
S	M	T	W	T	F	S
						1
2	3	4	5	6	7	8
9	10	11	12	13	14	15
16	17	18	19	20	21	22
23	24	25	26	27	28	29
30						

OCTOBER
S	M	T	W	T	F	S
	1	2	3	4	5	6
7	8	9	10	11	12	13
14	15	16	17	18	19	20
21	22	23	24	25	26	27
28	29	30	31			

NOVEMBER
S	M	T	W	T	F	S
				1	2	3
4	5	6	7	8	9	10
11	12	13	14	15	16	17
18	19	20	21	22	23	24
25	26	27	28	29	30	

DECEMBER
S	M	T	W	T	F	S
						1
2	3	4	5	6	7	8
9	10	11	12	13	14	15
16	17	18	19	20	21	22
23	24	25	26	27	28	29
30	31					

Notes for teachers
Objective: Read the time from calendars; use vocabulary related to time; know the number of days in each month. The final three sheets of the book are related to the New Year, as it follows so closely after Christmas. A surprising number of Y6 children find difficulty in remembering the order of the months of the year and the number of days in each month. This 2007 calendar can be used as the focus for discussion and can be compared with the 2008 calendar on Worksheet 43. What differences can be observed?

Andrew Brodie: Christmas Maths 9–11 © A & C Black Publishers Ltd. 2006　　　　　45

2008 Calendar

Name: Date:

JANUARY
S	M	T	W	T	F	S
		1	2	3	4	5
6	7	8	9	10	11	12
13	14	15	16	17	18	19
20	21	22	23	24	25	26
27	28	29	30	31		

FEBRUARY
S	M	T	W	T	F	S
					1	2
3	4	5	6	7	8	9
10	11	12	13	14	15	16
17	18	19	20	21	22	23
24	25	26	27	28	29	

MARCH
S	M	T	W	T	F	S
						1
2	3	4	5	6	7	8
9	10	11	12	13	14	15
16	17	18	19	20	21	22
23	24	25	26	27	28	29
30	31					

APRIL
S	M	T	W	T	F	S
		1	2	3	4	5
6	7	8	9	10	11	12
13	14	15	16	17	18	19
20	21	22	23	24	25	26
27	28	29	30			

MAY
S	M	T	W	T	F	S
				1	2	3
4	5	6	7	8	9	10
11	12	13	14	15	16	17
18	19	20	21	22	23	24
25	26	27	28	29	30	31

JUNE
S	M	T	W	T	F	S
1	2	3	4	5	6	7
8	9	10	11	12	13	14
15	16	17	18	19	20	21
22	23	24	25	26	27	28
29	30					

JULY
S	M	T	W	T	F	S
		1	2	3	4	5
6	7	8	9	10	11	12
13	14	15	16	17	18	19
20	21	22	23	24	25	26
27	28	29	30	31		

AUGUST
S	M	T	W	T	F	S
					1	2
3	4	5	6	7	8	9
10	11	12	13	14	15	16
17	18	19	20	21	22	23
24	25	26	27	28	29	30
31						

SEPTEMBER
S	M	T	W	T	F	S
	1	2	3	4	5	6
7	8	9	10	11	12	13
14	15	16	17	18	19	20
21	22	23	24	25	26	27
28	29	30				

OCTOBER
S	M	T	W	T	F	S
			1	2	3	4
5	6	7	8	9	10	11
12	13	14	15	16	17	18
19	20	21	22	23	24	25
26	27	28	29	30	31	

NOVEMBER
S	M	T	W	T	F	S
						1
2	3	4	5	6	7	8
9	10	11	12	13	14	15
16	17	18	19	20	21	22
23	24	25	26	27	28	29
30						

DECEMBER
S	M	T	W	T	F	S
	1	2	3	4	5	6
7	8	9	10	11	12	13
14	15	16	17	18	19	20
21	22	23	24	25	26	27
28	29	30	31			

Notes for teachers
Objective: Read the time from calendars; use vocabulary related to time; know the number of days in each month. What differences can be observed between this calendar for 2008 and the calendar for 2007? (2008 is, of course, a leap year.) What day of the week does each child's birthday fall on in 2007 and in 2008 – for some children there will be one day difference and for others there will be two days difference; can they explain why? Which day of the week does Christmas fall on in 2007 and 2008?

worksheet 44

My Calendar

Name: Date:

JANUARY
S	M	T	W	T	F	S

FEBRUARY
S	M	T	W	T	F	S

MARCH
S	M	T	W	T	F	S

APRIL
S	M	T	W	T	F	S

MAY
S	M	T	W	T	F	S

JUNE
S	M	T	W	T	F	S

JULY
S	M	T	W	T	F	S

AUGUST
S	M	T	W	T	F	S

SEPTEMBER
S	M	T	W	T	F	S

OCTOBER
S	M	T	W	T	F	S

NOVEMBER
S	M	T	W	T	F	S

DECEMBER
S	M	T	W	T	F	S

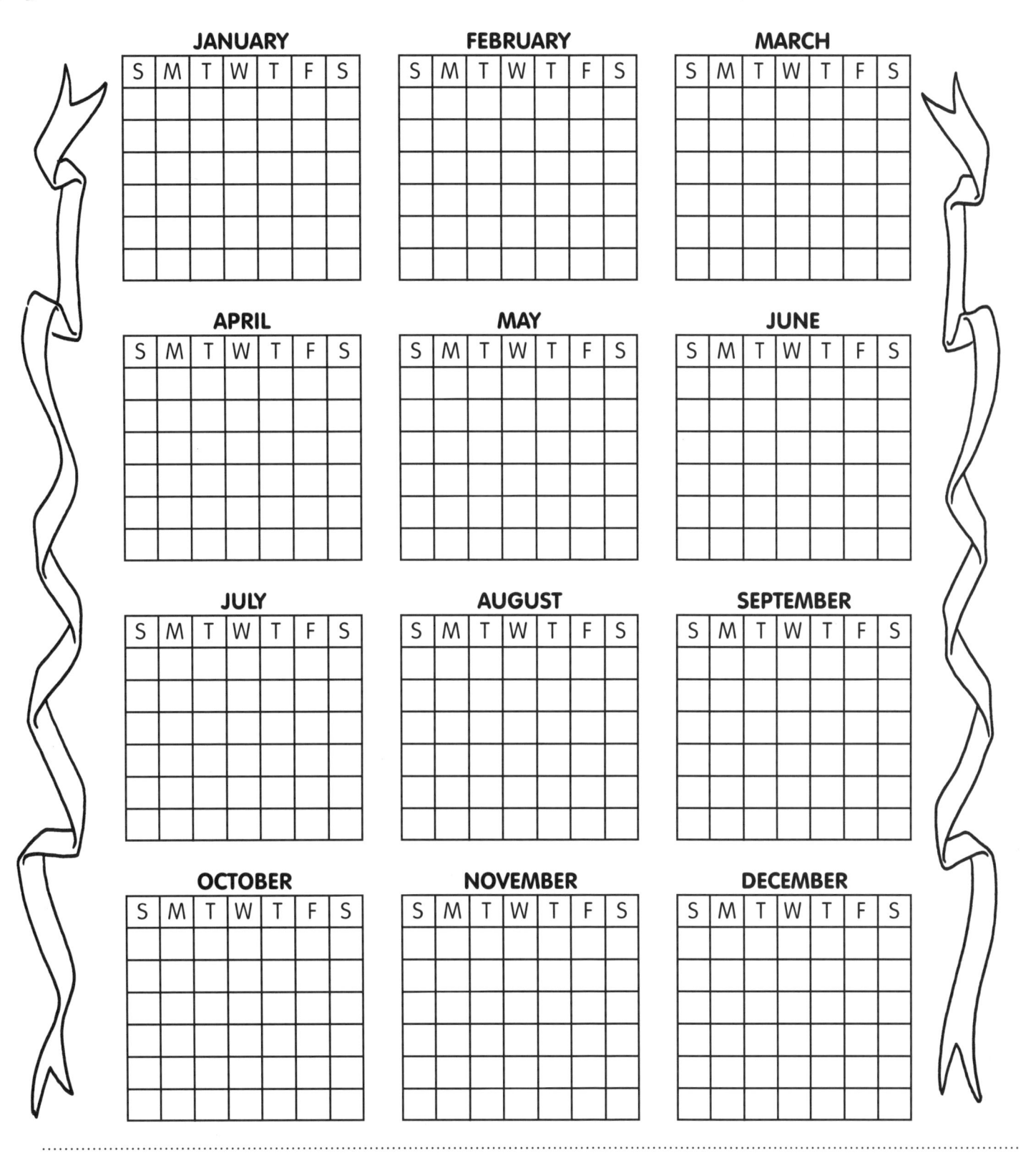

Notes for teachers
Objective: Read the time from calendars; use vocabulary related to time; know the number of days in each month. The children can prepare their own calendar for the new year. They may need some support in completing it as it is very easy to make a mistake, especially if the new year is a leap year. Show the children how to start January by writing the number 1 under the appropriate initial letter for the day of the week. The rest of the calendar should be able to flow from this starting point. The children may like to illustrate the edges of the calendar to reflect the season.

Andrew Brodie: Christmas Maths 9–11 © A & C Black Publishers Ltd. 2006

Answers

Worksheet 5
18,000 < books < 20,000
7,600 < skateboards < 7,700
9,990 < skates < 10,309
11,295 < board games < 12,700
12,300 < footballs < 14,432
3,999 < art sets < 4,999
6,000 < watches < 7,500
9,649 < electronic games < 9,651
15,000 < woolly hats < 17,000

Worksheet 6
Art sets	4,924	4,920	4,900	5,000
Watches	6,256	6,260	6,300	6,000
Skateboards	7,627	7,630	7600	8,000
Electronic games	9,650	9,650	9,700	10,000
Skates	10,308	10,310	10,300	10,000
Board games	11,498	11,500	11,500	11,000
Footballs	12,738	12,740	12,700	13,000
Woolly hats	16,249	16,250	16,200	16,000
Books	19,653	19,650	19,700	20,000

Worksheet 7
The extras of each item needed to reach 20,000 are as follows:
Board games 8,502   Art sets 15,076   Books 347
Electronic games 10,350   Skateboards 12,373
Footballs 7,262   Watches 13,744
Skates 9,692   Woolly hats 3,751

Worksheet 12
fairy: (6, 19)   small star: (8, 14)   big star: (3, 6)   candy cane: (5, 15)
snowman: (7, 17)   Father Christmas: (4, 12)

Worksheet 14
4 pm: 16.00   6 pm: 18.00   8 pm: 20.00
12 midnight: 00.00   7 am: 07.00   9 am: 09.00
10 am: 10.00   12 noon: 12.00

Worksheet 16
Fir Tree Lane   10, 13, 16, 19, 25, 28, 31, 34, 37
Sleigh Road   5, 11, 17, 23, 29, 35, 41, 47, 53, 59
December Street   24, 48, 72, 96, 120, 144, 168, 192, 216, 240
Snow Road   2, 11, 20, 29, 38, 47, 56, 65, 74, 83
Celebration Terrace   7, 11, 15, 19, 23, 27, 31, 35, 39, 43
Santa Street   8, 19, 30, 41, 52, 63, 74, 85, 96, 107

Worksheet 17
Zac $1\frac{3}{4}$ Kai $1\frac{1}{2}$ Lea $5\frac{2}{3}$ Ellie $6\frac{1}{2}$ Eve $4\frac{1}{10}$
Jack $1\frac{3}{8}$ Toru $2\frac{1}{2}$ Mel $3\frac{4}{5}$ Sita 4   Abe 3

Worksheet 18
Vixen $\frac{9}{10}$ Rudolph $\frac{1}{3}$ Dancer $\frac{4}{5}$ Prancer $\frac{4}{6}$ Blitzen $\frac{4}{14}$
Cupid $\frac{7}{10}$ Comet $\frac{5}{10}$ Donner $\frac{9}{15}$ Dasher $\frac{6}{8}$

Worksheet 19
1. 200 mins   **2.** 3 hrs 20 mins   **3.** 10.10 am
4. 1.30 pm   **5.** 2.15 pm

Worksheet 20
4 kg	160	2 hrs 40 mins	10 am	12.40 pm
4.5 kg	180	3 hrs	10 am	1 pm
5 kg	200	3 hrs 20 mins	10.30 am	1.50 pm
5.5 kg	220	3 hrs 40 mins	9.45 am	1.25 pm
6 kg	240	4 hrs	9.30 am	1.30 pm
6.5 kg	260	4 hrs 20 mins	9.40 am	2 pm
7 kg	280	4 hrs 40 mins	9.30 am	2.10 pm
7.5 kg	300	5 hrs	9 am	2 pm
8 kg	320	5 hrs 20 mins	8.55 am	2.15 pm
8.5 kg	340	5 hrs 40 mins	8 am	1.40 pm
9 kg	360	6 hrs	7.30 am	1.30 pm
9.5 kg	380	6 hrs 20 mins	7.40 am	2 pm
10 kg	400	6 hrs 40 mins	7.20 am	2 pm

Worksheet 24
6 Turkeys   6 x £12.75   £76.50
8 Strings of sausages   8 x £1.50   £12.00
4 kg Mixed fruit   4 x £3.60   £14.40
4 l Cranberry sauce   4 x £2.00   £8.00
5 Boxes of chocolates   5 x £3.00   £15.00

1. The total costs of all these ingredients was £125.90
2. The mean average cost per guest was £2.00

Worksheet 25
6 Turkeys   £76.50   7.65   £68.85
8 Strings of sausages   £12.00   £1.20   £10.80
4 kg Mixed fruit   £14.40   £1.44   £12.96
4 l Cranberry sauce   £8.00   £0.80   £7.20
5 Boxes of chocolates   £15.00   £1.50   £13.50

1. The total reduced cost was £113.31
2. The mean average has not changed.

Worksheet 26
Ice cream: 12 l   Custard: 200 ml   Soup: $\frac{1}{6}$ of a saucepan
Croutons: 3 kg   Sausages: 2   Sprouts: 360
Green beans: 125 g   Carrots: 125 g   Mince pies: 60

Worksheet 27
£45   £112.50   £157.50   £225   £270
£360   £450   £562.50   £1125   £1350

Worksheet 28
1. 132   **2.** 120   **3.** 126   **4.** 138   **5.** 84   **6.** 99
7. 104   **8.** 115   **9.** 103   **10.** 97   **11.** 82   **12.** 600

Worksheet 29
Bicycles	132	132 ÷ 6	22
Dolls	120	120 ÷ 6	20
Board games	126	126 ÷ 6	21
Footballs	138	138 ÷ 6	23
Skateboards	84	84 ÷ 6	14

The extra toys needed to reach 150 of each:
Bicycles 18   Dolls 30   Board games 24
Footballs 12   Skateboards 66

Worksheet 30
1. A and B: 1.79 m   A and I: 0.14 m   J and B: 4.09 m
    D and E: 3.09 m   F and C: 0.2 m   C and D: 0.31 m
    E and F: 2.58 m   B and C: 3.13 m   G and H: 1.38 m
    I and J: 2.44 m   F and G: 0.06 m   D and H: 1.83 m
2. 11.07 m   **3.** 9.07 m   **4.** 6.85 m
5. A: 4.02 m   B: 5.81 m   C: 2.68 m   D: 2.37 m   E: 5.46 m
    F: 2.88 m   G: 2.82 m   H: 4.2 m   I: 4.16 m   J: 1.72 m

Worksheet 37
1. a) 800 ml   **b)** 450 ml   **c)** 875 ml   **d)** 800 ml
2. 2.925 l   **3.** 1.75 l   **4.** 875 ml   **5.** 300 ml
6. £1.96   £2.55   £1.64   £3.85   £3.00   £1.26   £8.11

Worksheet 38
Festive Street   65p 65p 55p 33p 28p   Total = £2.46
Frosty Road   55p 55p 60p 55p 70p   Total = £2.95
Starlight Lane   28p 33p 70p 38p 65p   Total = £2.34
Winter Avenue   60p 65p 28p 33p 65p   Total = £2.51
Grand total = £10.26

Worksheet 39
1. £3.10   **2.** £2.70   **3.** £3.40   **4.** £27   **5.** £31
6. £34   **7.** £3400   **8.** £2700   **9.** £3100   **10.** £19 100
11. a) £13 700   **b)** £5730

Worksheet 41
1. 5   **2.** 9 + 16   **3.** 625   **4.** 1, 5, 25
5. 1 x 25 = 25   2 x 25 = 50   3 x 25 = 75   4 x 25 = 100
    5 x 25 = 125   6 x 25 = 150   7 x 25 = 175   8 x 25 = 200
    9 x 25 = 225   10 x 25 = 250
6. 979   997   889   898   988
7. 2 + 3 + 7 + 13   2 + 5 + 7 + 11   2 + 23
    3 + 5 + 17   5 + 7 + 13